THE ULTIMATE TEAM BUILDING FORMULA

HOW TO CREATE A LOYAL TEAM CULTURE, A ROCK-SOLID INFRASTRUCTURE, AND AN ARMY OF LEADERS WITHIN YOUR HOME-BASED BUSINESS ORGANIZATION

by Tracey Walker

Pretti-Fly Enterprises, LLC

Walker, Tracey

    The Ultimate Team Building Formula/by Tracey Walker

Tracey Walker

    ISBN: 978-0-9903895-0-7

Cover design and layout by HR Designz

Warning-Disclaimer
The purpose of this book is to educate and entertain. The author or publisher does not guarantee that anyone following the techniques, suggestions, tips, ideas, or strategies will become successful. The author and publisher shall have neither liability or responsibility to anyone with respect to any loss or damage caused, or alleged to be caused, directly or indirectly by the information contained in this book.

For Greg,

My love and inspiration

For Jasiah,

My precious gift from God

For Isaac, Kylah and Alexis,

I am eternally grateful to be blessed by you

For Mom & Dad,

My biggest fans and source of encouragement

For The Dream Team,

My family, my squad, and my motivation

Other Trainings and Resources By Tracey Walker

You can register for FREE access to these tools online at:

www.MyUniversityOfFreedom.com

Testimonials

"Tracey, as a team leader, you have taught me so many things simply through your actions. I have learned conflict resolution, coaching, speaking life into others, as well as the importance of the speed of implementation. You are a true professional with a heart of gold. It is definitely an honor to serve with you."

~ Valentino Crawford, www.TheGrowRichProject.com

"After fumbling in the home base business industry from 2006-2010 getting minimal results if any, I was ready to throw in the towel. It wasn't until I partnered with Tracey Walker in 2011 I started getting massive results. Following her mentoring and using her simple system, I have now become a better marketer, generating more leads, sponsoring more reps and making more money in my home base business. Thank you Tracey."

~ Shawn Johnson, www.SponsorMoreLeads.com

"Tracey Walker has absolutely been the catalyst to me seeing a massive increase in leads. As an internet marketer who struggled in the beginning, I know the value of mentorship. She is the best mentor I could have ever came across. She is an invaluable asset to my business and personal life."

~Roger Silvera, www.rogersilveraonline.com

"The leadership of Tracey Walker's has played a significant role in my life. Her knowledge of marketing is priceless and her real-world experiences are proof that when you make the decision to overcome the odds, you will. I am eternally grateful to have her as a mentor."

~ Ken Beckford

"Tracey Walker is a phenomenal leader. My outlook on life and business success has changed tremendously since being connected with Tracey. I always knew that I was destined for greatness but lacked the right mentorship and direction to help pull it out of me. Connecting with Tracey was definitely a divine appointment. She has deposited into to me such a strong sense of belief in my ability to live out my dreams. I am forever grateful for such a strong, driven and caring leader."

~ Sharron Mays, www.TheUpgradeCoachSpeaks.com

"Tracey Walker has literally changed my life. Her techniques to leadership build confidence and strength. After following the techniques taught by Tracey, I've not only improved in business yet also in my abilities to communicate with my children and others I love. She simply understands that success starts from the inside out and shared a blueprint that works."

~ Shalonda Gordon, www.ShalondaGordon.net

"Tracey has been a business mentor and coach for me for over five years and during that time my business has grown 20X more than when I was trying to do it all on my own. I count it a privilege to have her in my life."

~ Carlton Riddick, www.laptopriches.com

"As an engineer, I understand systems and what it takes to operate optimally. After examining Tracey Walker's organization and orchestrated leadership style, I was sold and knew she was a leader worth following."

~ Buihe Madu, www.buihemadu.com

"With virtually no home-based business experience, following Tracey Walkers program I was able to "break-even" inside of 3 months and parlay that success into a 5 figure income the following month. Tracey lights the path, all one needs to do to become successful is follow."

~ Matthew LoCicero

"Since applying the freedom formula Tracey Walker taught me, I have earned over $60,000+ in commissions from my home business. Prior to that, I never made more than $13,000 in a single year working a job as a frustrated college dropout."

~Brian Cain, www.CainBrian.com

"Tracey Walker, As a Phenomenal Leader of Leaders, the Masterful Methods you have taught time over time has help me to overcome the road blocks that were sabotaging my success and those very things I DO daily to overcome any challenge or roadblock that gets in the way of reaching my goals. Thank you Sis! You are loved...."

~ Anthony Polonio

"Prior to gaining Tracey Walker as my mentor and being apart of the Dream Team I was barely making enough money to pay my bill. Now through Tracey's leadership and dynamic training I was able to learn marketing skills that has helped me to define my target market and finally earn a nice residual income each month.

~ Lori Robertson, www.workwithlorirobertson.info

"Tracey Walker is one of the most authentic and exemplary leaders I have ever had the privilege to know and learn from! Because of her teachings and example, I have become more focused and effective in my business and have developed in my own leadership qualities as well. I am truly blessed to have her in my life! "

~ Emily Giuffre'

"Prior to using Tracey's Marketing Mastery 101 Training, I struggled in getting leads online. It wasn't until I "applied" what was taught in this course, that I started to see results in how I market my business online. This course taught me how to market to a specific group of people and become more confident about my message; allowing me to see an increase in the number of people that opt into my list of about 59%."

~ Simone Harvey, www.SingleParentPreneurs.com

Table of Contents

Introduction

The Ultimate Team Building Formula is jam-packed with all the information you need to successfully create and build the long-term team environment necessary in the field of home-based business to maximize profits. Once you are able to do this, consistently, you can build any business, with any product and be positioned to guarantee your own residual income increase.

From knowing how to setup a central location for your team to resolving and handling conflict internally, I reveal my exact 7-step system, to develop a stress-free, thriving and automated process to ensure your team grows, with or without you!

As an active participant in the home-based business industry I can tell you what works, what doesn't, what to do and what not to do, with precision.

I wrote this book to provide home-based business entrepreneurs with the step-by-step actions you need to build the team you know is possible. If you put my advice into action you can have the Ultimate Team inside of your company that is self-sustaining and that grows by leaps and bounds starting today!

1. In the Beginning

Upon graduating with my MBA in the fall of 1999 at the age of 23, I was $25,000 in debt, broke, and unemployed. It wasn't until the summer of 2000 when I found an energy trading position with a company in Atlanta, Georgia. During my time at this firm, I worked some pretty aggressive hours. I had four days on with 12-hour shifts, and then four days off. But here was the kicker; the first four days I worked 7a.m.-7p.m. and then after my four days off returned to work with my hours flip-flopped from 7p.m.-7a.m. for four days.

My body was constantly trying to adjust. Some days I ate lunch at midnight and other days at noon. I could not sleep and was tired most of the time. It was horrible, and I literally cried every day.

Unfortunately, the events of 9-11 took place; my company was greatly affected, as was the entire energy industry. A round of lay-offs began and I prayed to be part of that lucky bunch! Weird for most people to understand, I know…but still, it was my heart's desire.

On March 1, 2002, my wish came true.

I started building a real estate investment business and utilized my severance pay as well as my unemployment funds to market and generate leads off-line.

This was where I first discovered the road of entrepreneurship!

In an effort to assist homeowners who were facing foreclosure, I specialized in negotiating short sales. And let me tell you, I was so happy to be in control of my own life!

Then in July 2002 I got a call from my mom that changed everything. She told me she had been diagnosed with stage 4 lung cancer, and the doctors told her she had six months to live. So in August of the same year, I packed up my car and drove back to Chicago to take care of my mom. After 8 months of being diagnosed, my mother passed away. That was March 2, 2003, a day I will never forget.

This is a collage of photos with me, my mom, and my dad that my cousin assembled for me as a gift.

Wasn't she simply BEAUTIFUL!!!

After her passing, I swore I would make my business work no matter what. Working seemed to be all I had to live for. Then in July, my then boyfriend's mother was diagnosed with cancer as well. So, we went another year of caring for a cancer patient before she too passed on June 4, 2004. Everything seemed to be happening so fast.

Later that year we became engaged to get married and did so in 2005.

My now ex-husband and I built a 3500 sq. ft. home from the ground up in the suburbs of Chicago. We bought luxury cars, including a Mercedes Benz CL500 and the Hummer H2. We bought stupid stuff like jewelry and went out of town quite a bit. We were making anywhere between $30k and $90k per month (we would close on average 3 deals a month netting as much as $30k each.) We were on top of the world and only in our late 20s! We blew money, stupidly, and we did not save like we should have. We never thought the season of bliss would end. However, life would surely teach us otherwise.

Negotiating short sales was our niche. We supported 3 owners and 3 employees. Our only income or cash flow occurred when a closing happened. While there might have been a few big closings one month, if there were no closing the next month, there was no income that month. We always depended on the "next big deal" to pull us into positive cash flow again. Our income was extremely volatile and soon I discovered how residual income would be ideal to help us between deals; something we could rely on.

However, we refused to be landlords—that was not an option. So, we continued to focus on closing more deals.

Even though we knew something in our business model had to change, things were going strong up until 2006 when the mortgage laws and overall housing market began to shift.

Unable to close deals in our pipeline, no money was coming in. It seemed like my business just grinded to a halt.

Soon, *my* home went into foreclosure, my cars went into repossession, my electricity, cable, and gas were all rigged. My life was in shambles, and I believed I had to continue to fool the world. While I walked around with my "happy mask" on in the daytime, I cried myself to sleep every night.

I knew I had to do something, and I needed a steady income.

2. The Awakening

In January of 2007, I was introduced to the industry of Network Marketing by a good college buddy of mine. He happened to be a mortgage broker who was also facing the music of not making money like we did in the "good ole' days."

After seeing my first home presentation, I signed up right away. I just knew I was going to hit the ball right out of the park in no time flat. I listened to my thriving up-line and decided to follow their lead.

The Network Marketing Grind

I got right to work. I made cold calls, performed hundreds of presentations, and passed out flyers and business cards at every networking event. I bought booths at huge expos and took a few hours of my time every day to prospect in the shopping malls. I bugged the crap out of my friends and family and was a chronic "phone booker."

As one of our team's main presenters, I had to show up whether guests did or not. And in Chicago, even the weather didn't stop the show. We hosted training sessions two or three times a week. I presented the opportunity on Tuesdays and Thursdays (alongside the WealthAngels; a trio of us who became the branded presentation team within our Chicago-area organization). I trained at Super Saturday trainings and traveled with new reps to the home office every couple of weeks.

The "I'll Do It" Syndrome

Somewhere in my life, I learned that if something was going to be done right, I personally had to do it. (What a counter-productive philosophy). So, when new reps would join my team, I often felt compelled to raise my hand and volunteer doing the presenting for them.

I was in workhorse mode just to reach my weekly bonuses while constantly being plagued with people falling off auto-ship. I partnered with a few people in my up-line in hiring a call center to reactivate inactive members and still, I remained stuck... just under qualification for next leadership for 6 months. I was totally aggravated and it was then that I accepted that I could not do this alone or even keep trying to. I recognized teamwork was better than me doing it all.

Lone-Star Reps

I never understood why people would join but not come to training. It was baffling to me then, and quite frankly, it still is. As a result, new reps didn't know how to get started and many were left dangling in the wind not knowing they had a team.

I started digging for a way to systemize the start-up process and decided to create a new member start-up guide from scratch. It was an awesome idea, I thought.

As I found myself at the copy shop each week, spending hundreds of dollars in replicating the workbook, I soon found that this method was too costly to sustain and yet, ineffective at keeping new reps "in the know."

Searching for Love in all the Wrong Places

As hard as I was working, I had no way of measuring what was actually working and what was not. I tapped into trainings of other team leaders and recommended my team study these leaders too. We were all over the place, with no focus, no real action plan, and no way to even identify the "right way" even if it stared us right in the face. My passion was fading fast and my grip on business was slipping…again.

What's Behind That Curtain

Frequently, I would reach out to my up-line for answers while on a quest to find out what was really going on and what they were doing to make $40K and $50K or more per month. I just knew there was "a secret" that they weren't telling me. I learned about "deals," positions, and agreements between leaders and discovered they truly didn't have a clear plan either.

I offered suggestions that we try new marketing ideas such as online marketing and expand our vision on marketing a bit. Even still, not much changed.

I felt in my heart there was a better approach to marketing and building a company for the residual benefits, but I also knew doing things the old way was really wasting my time. I decided at that point...enough is enough!

I could either give up and quit, or learn the skills required to be successful in this industry. That was when I began searching for ways to duplicate myself via video and market on the internet. I did some research, found a mentor to follow, learned a few techniques and made a few bucks here and there as I applied what I was learning.

But what happened to me next, I totally didn't expect.

3. The Dream

In March of 2008, the millionaire mentor I found helped me see why my business was failing. He gave me a different perspective on how I should be marketing and revealed to me that I could generate leads online, enroll new reps into my business on autopilot, and do it all without having to even speak to anyone first. His name was Daegan Smith!

From that day forward, I began to see changes in me, my strategy, my lead count, and my bank account.

Within three months of meeting Daegan and working with him, I was offered an opportunity to be a featured co-author in "The Power of Leadership" Book Series from a guy who spotted me on MySpace. I accepted the offer and contributed to the project. This platform not only gave me the ability to appear in writing amongst the ranks of many New York Times bestselling authors such as Ivan Misner and Ben Gay III, but I now held the title "published author."

Over the next two years, I began to master several online marketing strategies and use tools such as video marketing and blogging for leverage and duplication. This helped me build teams on autopilot while always remembering the Lone-star reps. I joined several different businesses during this time and picked up more effective methods along the way to keep the team working and plugged in.

Through my own trial and error, I developed a basic system, a seven-step formula and structure for team building, training, and developing a culture. I used this exact formula to become the top female income producer in two online businesses where I personally enrolled over 900 distributors all online.

In the first of those two companies, I became a top 10 producer of all-time in the system as well as the #1 Female Recruiter of All-Time. I achieved the L4 Leadership Level (out of 6 levels) and was invited to be a keynote speaker at two international marketing conferences. I was definitely making my way to getting my life back on-track.

Simultaneously in my real estate business, the people who worked for me did so mainly because they needed a paycheck. I was the boss in that traditional business model and could fire and hire at will. However, in network marketing, I was not the boss and could not lead using the fear of cutting someone's check. Nor could I fire or hire. I had to lead by doing and inspire by example only.

I truly loved the ability to get paid every week between deals. I learned that making 1% of 100 people's efforts was far better than relying only on 100% of my own efforts. This income model was the exact thing I had been looking for all that time.

Live the Dream I Conference (2010)

In Oct 2009, we moved back down to Atlanta, as I figured a change in environment would be another springboard in this journey of success. And in many ways, it was. From the business perspective, I created my first free training course: "The 5-Day Marketing M.A.P." as well as my first blogging product, "Be Blog Savvy."

Be Blog Savvy launched in February 2010 and generated

over $10k the first 12 hours in the market place. It was my first time ever making 5-figures in 1 day online and became a benchmark for me regarding what was possible.

Yet, as my business began to grow, my marriage; well, not so much. And to make a long story short, we ultimately divorced after 7 years.

So, I dived back into my work. It served as a distraction, as a way for me to focus on something other than my current circumstances.

After a short while, I began to feel burned out because I couldn't wrap my mind around one thing in particular. Having an online business was something people claimed they wanted, but did not appear as serious about mastering it as I was. I was once again providing all the training and all the support I could for those who requested assistance; however, it seemed like the harder I worked to help, the lesser the results became. This was strange to me, because in my heart, I really wanted these internet entrepreneurs to succeed.

Since many of them were not, I started to feel out of place, not really knowing how to fit in the marketplace anymore, or if I even provided the value I once did.

I spoke to my online colleagues and friends and so many of them were experiencing the same burn-out. As I would sit with my head in the palms of my hands on many occasions, all I could think was "now what am I gonna do?"

Then something happened…as it always seemed to.

On October 26, 2011, I had a conversation with two of my friends, David Wood and David Sharpe. They shared with me some information about a new company they were starting in an effort to help more people by paying out higher percentages in the commissions. I asked Dave Wood what the primary product would be, and he responded that the business would be based around the platform of blogging.

"Yes!" I thought. After all, blogging was my favorite strategy, and it was in-part responsible for helping me to brand myself, build teams, have 5-figure income months, and speak onstage to live audiences. Now, an automated blogging system was going to be available to others. I signed up that day to partner with the Daves, got "all-in," and began to market like never before.

By May 31, 2012 (approximately 7 months later) I had earned over $98,000 in commissions from this "new little company."

The people I had recruited were on fire.

I started witnessing others either have their first sale ever online, their first $1k day online, or their first recruit to sign up on auto-pilot.

I knew this worked immediately, because I wasn't the only one doing it. Hundreds of others were experiencing results too.

At the very first company event, June 2012, I was awarded a "big" check representing commissions earned from Oct 2011-May 2012. You can see my team and me celebrating in the photo.

Disclaimer

Results not typical. Please see our income disclosure at

http://disclaimer.traceywalkeronline.com/

Today I continue to speak at events, train, conduct webinars, recruit, build teams, make money, and do it all from home on my laptop computer.

My life is phenomenal, and I am grateful for each and every experience God has allowed me to have.

Nothing Stopped Me!

Nothing I faced in my life killed me. Nothing was the end of the world. And nothing stopped me from pushing forward. Not the foreclosure, not the down-turn in the market, not losing my job, not the repossessions, and not the divorce. In fact, all those things made me stronger, more confident, and toughened up my rhino skin.

So now you know about my past, where I've traveled from, and some awesome accomplishments I've had thus far. Allow me to now share with you where I'm traveling to and why I decided to write a book and reveal my successful team building formula.

My areas of expertise are: Social Media, Video Marketing, Blogging, and Team Building. I enjoy showing other network marketers how to use many of these internet strategies to help generate leads and enroll more reps into their businesses.

I am driven each day to do better today than I did yesterday. And I can only hope that through my "EntrepreDOER"

Duplicate

Show your leaders how to duplicate this exact system. Since this system works treat it as a franchise. Make sure your leadership council and leadership mastermind has this book and promotes duplication several levels down. This keeps teams within the team operating the same way and helps build familiarity and confidence because of the consistency of the message.

Then let them fly!

I personally feel as though we have created a "fantasy" team in the Dream Team utilizing the Ultimate Team Building Formula. It took me quite sometime to tweak and modify this formula so that it produced results.

Now that it is proven, I am excited to have had the opportunity to share this winning formula with you so that you too can create the team of your dreams.

If I was able to do it, so can you!

About the Author

 Tracey Walker is an expert home-based business entrepreneur and internet marketer. In just a little over a year online, she became a leading force in the Network Marketing training industry and has achieved top producer/Top Female Income Producer status in both of the internet marketing programs she has chosen to be an affiliate of.

Prior to joining the home-based business arena, Tracey was a highly influential and successful real estate investor specializing in pre-foreclosures and negotiating short sales. It was the downturn in the market that was the catalyst in her being exposed to and participating in the network marketing industry.

During her first years in network marketing, Tracey was an offline presenter for her previous network marketing companies. In this role, she not only led her own organization, but also trained the core team in Chicago of over 2000 distributors. It was here where she honed in on coaching and training serious network marketers to be successful.

This is a collage of photos with me, my mom, and my dad that my cousin assembled for me as a gift.

Wasn't she simply BEAUTIFUL!!!

After her passing, I swore I would make my business work no matter what. Working seemed to be all I had to live for. Then in July, my then boyfriend's mother was diagnosed with cancer as well. So, we went another year of caring for a cancer patient before she too passed on June 4, 2004. Everything seemed to be happening so fast.

Later that year we became engaged to get married and did so in 2005.

My now ex-husband and I built a 3500 sq. ft. home from the ground up in the suburbs of Chicago. We bought luxury cars, including a Mercedes Benz CL500 and the Hummer H2. We bought stupid stuff like jewelry and went out of town quite a bit. We were making anywhere between $30k and $90k per month (we would close on average 3 deals a month netting as much as $30k each.) We were on top of the world and only in our late 20s! We blew money, stupidly, and we did not save like we should have. We never thought the season of bliss would end. However, life would surely teach us otherwise.

Negotiating short sales was our niche. We supported 3 owners and 3 employees. Our only income or cash flow occurred when a closing happened. While there might have been a few big closings one month, if there were no closing the next month, there was no income that month. We always depended on the "next big deal" to pull us into positive cash flow again. Our income was extremely volatile and soon I discovered how residual income would be ideal to help us between deals; something we could rely on.

3. The Dream

In March of 2008, the millionaire mentor I found helped me see why my business was failing. He gave me a different perspective on how I should be marketing and revealed to me that I could generate leads online, enroll new reps into my business on autopilot, and do it all without having to even speak to anyone first. His name was Daegan Smith!

From that day forward, I began to see changes in me, my strategy, my lead count, and my bank account.

Within three months of meeting Daegan and working with him, I was offered an opportunity to be a featured co-author in "The Power of Leadership" Book Series from a guy who spotted me on MySpace. I accepted the offer and contributed to the project. This platform not only gave me the ability to appear in writing amongst the ranks of many New York Times bestselling authors such as Ivan Misner and Ben Gay III, but I now held the title "published author."

Over the next two years, I began to master several online marketing strategies and use tools such as video marketing and blogging for leverage and duplication. This helped me build teams on autopilot while always remembering the Lone-star reps. I joined several different businesses during this time and picked up more effective methods along the way to keep the team working and plugged in.

Through my own trial and error, I developed a basic system, a seven-step formula and structure for team building, training, and developing a culture. I used this exact formula to become the top female income producer in two online businesses where I personally enrolled over 900 distributors all online.

In the first of those two companies, I became a top 10 producer of all-time in the system as well as the #1 Female Recruiter of All-Time. I achieved the L4 Leadership Level (out of 6 levels) and was invited to be a keynote speaker at two international marketing conferences. I was definitely making my way to getting my life back on-track.

Simultaneously in my real estate business, the people who worked for me did so mainly because they needed a paycheck. I was the boss in that traditional business model and could fire and hire at will. However, in network marketing, I was not the boss and could not lead using the fear of cutting someone's check. Nor could I fire or hire. I had to lead by doing and inspire by example only.

I truly loved the ability to get paid every week between deals. I learned that making 1% of 100 people's efforts was far better than relying only on 100% of my own efforts. This income model was the exact thing I had been looking for all that time.

Live the Dream I Conference (2010)

In Oct 2009, we moved back down to Atlanta, as I figured a change in environment would be another springboard in this journey of success. And in many ways, it was. From the business perspective, I created my first free training course: "The 5-Day Marketing M.A.P." as well as my first blogging product, "Be Blog Savvy."

Be Blog Savvy launched in February 2010 and generated

over $10k the first 12 hours in the market place. It was my first time ever making 5-figures in 1 day online and became a benchmark for me regarding what was possible.

Yet, as my business began to grow, my marriage; well, not so much. And to make a long story short, we ultimately divorced after 7 years.

So, I dived back into my work. It served as a distraction, as a way for me to focus on something other than my current circumstances.

After a short while, I began to feel burned out because I couldn't wrap my mind around one thing in particular. Having an online business was something people claimed they wanted, but did not appear as serious about mastering it as I was. I was once again providing all the training and all the support I could for those who requested assistance; however, it seemed like the harder I worked to help, the lesser the results became. This was strange to me, because in my heart, I really wanted these internet entrepreneurs to succeed.

Since many of them were not, I started to feel out of place, not really knowing how to fit in the marketplace anymore, or if I even provided the value I once did.

I spoke to my online colleagues and friends and so many of them were experiencing the same burn-out. As I would sit with my head in the palms of my hands on many occasions, all I could think was "now what am I gonna do?"

Then something happened…as it always seemed to.

On October 26, 2011, I had a conversation with two of my friends, David Wood and David Sharpe. They shared with me some information about a new company they were starting in an effort to help more people by paying out higher percentages in the commissions. I asked Dave Wood what the primary product would be, and he responded that the business would be based around the platform of blogging.

"Yes!" I thought. After all, blogging was my favorite strategy, and it was in-part responsible for helping me to brand myself, build teams, have 5-figure income months, and speak onstage to live audiences. Now, an automated blogging system was going to be available to others. I signed up that day to partner with the Daves, got "all-in," and began to market like never before.

By May 31, 2012 (approximately 7 months later) I had earned over $98,000 in commissions from this "new little company."

The people I had recruited were on fire.

I started witnessing others either have their first sale ever online, their first $1k day online, or their first recruit to sign up on auto-pilot.

I knew this worked immediately, because I wasn't the only one doing it. Hundreds of others were experiencing results too.

At the very first company event, June 2012, I was awarded a "big" check representing commissions earned from Oct 2011-May 2012. You can see my team and me celebrating in the photo.

EMP⬤WER NETWORK

June 6, 2012

PAY TO THE ORDER OF: Tracey Walker

$ 91,850.

Ninety One Thousand Eight Hundred and Fifty DOLLARS

Commissions Earned

Disclaimer

Results not typical. Please see our income disclosure at

http://disclaimer.traceywalkeronline.com/

Today I continue to speak at events, train, conduct webinars, recruit, build teams, make money, and do it all from home on my laptop computer.

My life is phenomenal, and I am grateful for each and every experience God has allowed me to have.

Nothing Stopped Me!

Nothing I faced in my life killed me. Nothing was the end of the world. And nothing stopped me from pushing forward. Not the foreclosure, not the down-turn in the market, not losing my job, not the repossessions, and not the divorce. In fact, all those things made me stronger, more confident, and toughened up my rhino skin.

So now you know about my past, where I've traveled from, and some awesome accomplishments I've had thus far. Allow me to now share with you where I'm traveling to and why I decided to write a book and reveal my successful team building formula.

My areas of expertise are: Social Media, Video Marketing, Blogging, and Team Building. I enjoy showing other network marketers how to use many of these internet strategies to help generate leads and enroll more reps into their businesses.

I am driven each day to do better today than I did yesterday. And I can only hope that through my "EntrepreDOER" lay I continue to speak at events, train, conduct webinars,

ild teams, make money, and do it all from home on my

nputer.

life is phenomenal, and I am grateful for each and every

God has allowed me to have.

hing Stopped Me !

hing I faced in my life killed me. Nothing was the end of

And nothing stopped me from pushing forward. Not

ure, not the down-turn in the market, not losing my job,

ossessions, and not the divorce. In fact, all those things

tronger, more confident, and toughened up my rhino

w you know about my past, where I've traveled from,

wesome accomplishments I've had thus far. Allow me

e with you where I'm traveling to and why I decided to

and reveal my successful team building formula.

reas of expertise are: Social Media, Video Marketing,

d Team Building. I enjoy showing other network

w to use many of these internet strategies to help

s and enroll more reps into their businesses.

driven each day to do better today than I did

nd I can only hope that through my "EntrepreDOER"

Discla

Results not typical. Please s

http://disclaimer.traceyv

To

re—cruit, bu

la_ptop cor

My

ex_perience

Not

Not

the— world.

the— foreclos

not— the rep

ma—de me s

skin.

So n

and some a

to now shar

write— a book

My a

Blogging, a

mark—eters h

gener—ate lead

I am

yester—day. A

(thanks Buihe Madu for this phrase) actions and attitudes, that I inspire you to take action and never give up as well.

I truly believe that most people in network marketing have failed due to the lack of "information age" training provided in the industry by "sponsors" and "up-lines."

There are very few people who know how to utilize the internet — modern marketing methods — effectively.

Fortunately, this is my skill and my niche, and that is what I offer you. My goal is to help as many network marketers as I can to succeed by not just teaching these strategies, but by implementing them for you to see them in action.

My dream has always been to be successful, yes, but I've also desired to have a thriving team; a team that had a roadmap to follow, a team that was making money and profiting in their businesses, and a team that could function without the "hand-holding" that we see so often in our industry. And today that is exactly what I have been blessed with, literally, a Dream Team!

To give you more insight on why I believe I have a Dream Team here are some examples of what is happening for us:

I have personally sponsored over 900 reps and have earned over $700,000 in 19 months.

My top producer, Nicole Cooper, earned over $250,000 in her first 10 months, even after battling post-partum depression.

Shalonda Gordon, a single mother of two, who has worked with me since 2010, finally cracked the code and is earning enough each month to pay her mortgage and all of her household bills with her commissions.

Adrian Hines was able to quit his job by the age of 33 and replace his salaried income with his earnings from his homebusiness.

Apple Daniels, a mother of three small children, was able to upgrade her family car from a small 4-door Mitsubishi, to an Infiniti SUV where all three of the car seats fit safely.

Brian Cain, a 21-year-old who dropped out of college twice, is now experiencing the leverage of having $1k days and $3k days each month.

Roger Silvera, a financial planner, has gone from struggling to generate leads online to generating over 70 leads per day!

Buihe Madu, an engineer but complete internet newbie, has gone from over analyzing the processes we teach to implementing them and allowing his creativity in marketing to step out and help him make sales on auto-pilot.

Carlton Riddick, a former broke internet marketer, has now realized the power of focusing on one business at a time and how using a highly converting system that pays 100% commissions can actually make him more money than if he promoted ten products.

And there are thousands of more stories like these within our team.

I firmly believe you can see this same type of success, too, if you apply the techniques I teach in this book.

So, as you continue to read the pages within, I am going to show you step-by-step how I built one of the highest retentive, duplicating, lucrative, loyal, and family-culture based teams in our industry, The Dream Team, which has set a new standard and given me the ability to manifest my dream of having a successful and profitable team.

4. Step One:

Create a Home-Base

"There's no place like home."

In the regular world, when you think of the phrase 'home base,' what do you initially picture? Maybe you see a place that you consider safe, or maybe you envision someplace where everyone is of the same mind or committed to the same mission like a military base. Well, in the online network marketing world, when your intent is to build a huge team, and one that duplicates, you can virtually create a 'home base' environment through using online tools and community based platforms. This is where you build your brand, your soldiers, your leaders, and your community.

Your home base also serves as the hub where you post and distribute pertinent content and material to the team. The key thing is that you need to have complete control over the content, be able to easily administer, add and remove functionalities, and allow interactive components for members. All this needs to be customizable, yet cost effective.

Since getting started online, I have used Ning.com to accomplish this. Ning is an online platform where you can create your own custom social network. Ning offers you the ability to build a community website with a tailored appearance and feel. You can allow photo and video uploads, create forums and blogs, and integrate with Facebook, Google, Twitter, and Yahoo! Estimates are that Ning currently hosts over 100,000 social websites.

What I really love about using a platform like Ning, is that it can easily be duplicated by the leaders that emerge on your team. There is no technical mumbo jumbo to know, there is no website code to have to master, there is no cost to try it, or anything complicated about getting a Ning network up and running.

Once you have opened a Ning.com account, choose a layout template and structure that is easy to follow. You want to limit the tabs in your menu bar to only what is necessary. Include a chat function and allow members to post videos and pictures so they get to know one another and learn about their similarities. Enable the commenting feature too. This gives all of your members a chance to communicate with one another and feel like there is "someone there to talk to" while building a business from home. Lastly, be sure to activate the group and event features so members dwell amongst others with like interests as well as stay abreast of activities and their dates.

Quick Start Tips for Ning:

1. Sign up to become a Ning.com member.

2. Log into Ning with your email address and password.

3. See the box to name your new social network and assign a URL. Come up with a descriptive and creative name for your new social network. You can use a shortened version of the name as the URL box. Then create your network.

4. Choose your functionalities.

- You can decide if your social networking site will be private or public, or by invitation only.

- Tagline: Your site can have a tagline or subtitle.

- Description: Tell visitors what your site is about, what they will find, and what to do next.

- Keywords: Choose words and phrases that best describe your site for people to use in a search about your site or products.

- Icon: You can choose a picture or graphic that describes you or the site and gets attention.

Be Unique and Exclusive

There is value in being unique and having exclusivity. My Ning network is private and is only accessible by members of our team. No guests or prospects can gain access. Period! To replicate this for yourself, create a member approval process and format your settings so that each new person who attempts to join your network must first answer "secret questions" that only people on your team would have the answer to. Do not make the link to your Ning public or searchable by the search engines. That way, only those who receive the network link directly from you or their sponsor will ever see that your network exists.

Create Initiatives

Set monthly themes and create webinars or training content around your themes. Urge members to take advantage of these additional resources.

What I did was choose a different theme for each month. For example, January would've been Financial Fitness Month. Upon that theme, our team created 1-2 trainings based on financial fitness, recorded them, and made them available for replay for all members on the Ning.

When your team realizes that you are serious and have things organized like a real business should, you'll notice how they begin to look forward to these types of events that have nothing to do with enrolling people so to speak, but more so with being a successful entrepreneur overall.

Formulate Your Mission Statement

Make no mistake about it, you are a business. And, you want your team to know they are part of a business. A mission statement will help signal this to your team.

When I was in business school, every corporation I studied—or had the opportunity to intern with—had a mission statement. Thus, it only made sense to me to form one for our team/business/organization so that we would all be focused on the same goal/mission and row in the same direction at all times.

Now, a mission statement can be simple, though it needs to convey your purpose, vision, and expectations. This is paramount for your team. The mission statement is the guiding principle that explains who you are, where you want to go, and how you will get there.

The greater your mission, the simpler your statement can be.

A well-written mission statement can be as short as a sentence or two. Here is Coca Cola's mission statement: "To refresh the world..." That says it all in four words.

You do not need to fill your mission statement with fluff words. Be direct and to the point to create a clear path for your team to follow.

A great mission statement will motivate your team and add focus for all the initiatives.

Here is the exact mission statement I created for my team in full:

"*The **mission of The Dream Team**, powered by Empower Network, is to assemble like-minded, positive entrepreneurs, from varying fields of expertise and knowledge, and **provide them with the life, personal development and marketing skills** absolutely necessary to achieve massive profits funneling into wealth through the internet marketing portal.*

Our vision is to empower business owners**, and increase the personal economies of our members, internationally, not only through our valuable and extensive network, but also through our programs, trainings, tools and events within the first 90 days of membership. As a community of internet marketing professionals, **we aim to assist in the creation of

the lifestyles desired by our members and hereby commit to breathing life into the dreams of those who truly desire freedom!"

Mission Statement Elements

A mission statement is an opportunity to express your uniqueness, convey your vision, and communicate your core values.

A mission statement has three basic components:

1. Vision
2. Mission
3. Core Values

Vision – Your vision is the mental picture of your expectation, what you want to accomplish.

Your vision statement should be concise. Make this a memorable statement that reflects exactly where you are going and easy for your team to memorize. You want to motivate your team with your vision and have them focusing toward achievement.

Mission - A mission statement is about how you will realize your vision. These statements often begin with the word "To." This statement is connected to the vision statement and should also be simple and direct.

Core Values - Core values define the principles and values of your business.

There is no reason to get caught up and frustrated about creating your mission statement. While they can be challenging to craft out at the beginning, they are not written in stone and you can modify your statement later if needed.

If you go back and look at my mission statement again, you should now be able to recognize these three components within its text.

Goals and Objectives

After you have established your vision, mission, and core values, develop the goals and objectives to achieve your vision.

This is extremely important!

The reason is because as the leader, you must know where you are going. Likewise, others deserve to know where you are going as well so they can decide whether they want to go there with you or not.

So take the time to do this just as a multi-millionaire or billionaire would do. Remember, how you do anything is how you do everything.

Goals: Integrate your mission and goals with your vision. Goals are milestones on the way to your vision. Examples of goals:

- To improve profitability
- To increase efficiency
- To recruit more team members
- To provide better customer service
- To improve training

A goal should fit your vision, mission, and values, be easy to understand and flexible enough to be adaptable if needed.

Do not set more goals than are absolutely needed or any that can conflict with other goals. Remember that goals are stepping stones, so design them to be reached and in sequence.

Do you see the goals in my mission statement?

Here's a hint:

"increase the personal economies of our members, internationally..."

"...to assist in the creation of the lifestyles desired by our members *and hereby commit to breathing life into the dreams of those who truly desire freedom."*

Objectives: Objectives are designed to be specific, quantifiable, and time-sensitive statements of what you will do and when. Objectives are the stepping stones along the path to achieving your goals.

Objectives should help you measure your progress toward your goals. Often several objectives can be created to help you meet each goal. Each objective needs a quantifiable outcome to be completed by a set deadline.

On our team, we have a very specific objective, which happens to be mentioned within our mission statement:

"...not only through our valuable and extensive network, but also through our programs, trainings, tools and events within the first 90 days of membership."

With an objective of helping our team members increase their income in their 1st 90 days, it pushes us as a team to get people started right, to help them get positioned properly so they have maximum earning potential, and encourage them to never give up as others have been successful using our same plan of action.

Create and Upload a Welcome Video

I've found that as new reps enroll into my organization, me speaking on a video, welcoming them to the team, creates a more personal relationship with them. As a result, more often than not, it's easier to move my new people through the getting started process.

In addition, a good welcome video is far more enticing than mere text.

The welcome video will allow you to immediately connect with new team members and build rapport. People like to see who they are working with and feel like they will belong. You can easily achieve this for yourself and your team by making a video and use text and graphics where possible. If you do not want to use video or are just a little gun shy right now, record an audio welcome message and at least include your picture for people to see as they listen.

During your video message, you can briefly explain how to navigate your site and provide consistent and systematic information on what action they need to take next.

The key benefit to you by doing this is leverage.

New members feel welcome, become informed, and learn

what to do all while you are off doing something else.

Tips for Creating a Welcome Video

Give Value: Start by thanking the new person for joining and welcome them to the team. Continue by letting them know that what you offer can't be found anywhere else and that they are in the right place.

Your Uniqueness: Express why you and your team are unique.

Include a Call to Action: Tell people what to do next, i.e. Heading over to the 10-step Fast Start Guide and begin with step #1.

Script Tips: Your welcome video should avoid time sensitive statements and information. Your script should flow like a conversation. You want to be and sound natural, not like you are giving a speech. Sometimes having someone there to speak to while you are taping can help. Be sure to know your script so that you can speak the words rather than merely read them. What's even better is if you can speak from the heart without a written script in the first place.

Trust me, your new member watching will be able to feel your sincerity.

Appearance: For the best production, wear light colored clothing and avoid solid white, plaids or stripes and anything too bright such as red or orange.

Use the Best Sound Available: Now don't get me wrong, you do not have to be a guru sound professional with all the up-to-date sound equipment used by Hollywood productions. However, make sure you sound clear and crisp. The easier it is to hear you, the better off your new member will be.

Use a Tripod: A moving or shaking video is annoying.

Avoid Moving the Camera Around, Panning, or Zooming: Your video is only two to five minutes. Too much moving or different screen shots can be distracting. Hold shots for about 10 seconds each.

Edit: Editing gives you the opportunity to pick the best shots and eliminate any mistakes or errors you made during the recording. You do not have to be perfect by any means. Just edit out what you don't want.

5. Step Two:

Establishing the Front Line

"Interdependent people combine their own efforts with the efforts of others to achieve their greatest success." - **Stephen Covey**

Team Building

Building a team requires a hierarchy and well defined roles. Likewise, I used my corporate experience once again and decided to create "board of directors" or what I like to call, a "leadership council" made up of people with varying skills and strengths can help my team grow and develop faster.

At the very beginning, after only having about 10-20 people on my team I defined six to eight leadership positions and appointed leaders to each. I also made sure men and women were both represented.

I incorporated my mission statement with my leadership council's purpose, discussed each role, the corresponding tasks, my expectations, and the rewards with each leader.

The roles were simple and easy to understand so that most anyone can perform in each position if adjustments ever needed to be made.

Overall, the leadership council is your advocate team. Make sure they understand and work for the greater good of the team. Leadership council members must subjugate their personal beliefs (not ethics) in favor of the team vision. When members are unwilling to make this sacrifice, infighting can occur, trust is lost, and your momentum suffers.

Creating a successful front-line does take time. Though this can be accomplished in as little as a few weeks, work will be required to optimize your team and this will not happen overnight. The availability of members, their motivation, and how organized your structure is will all contribute to the time required for your council to develop.

Building a front-line requires assessment. Here are the three steps I use in leadership council evaluation/selection:

1. Evaluate the skills and needs of each potential council member.

Meet or communicate with each potential member and ask the following questions:

- What are your strengths and weaknesses?
- What are your personal interests?
- What is your primary motivation? What is your secondary motivation? Because many people will say their primary motivation is money, the question about a secondary motivation will often provide you with their true motivation.
- What do you believe you can contribute to not only the council but the team as a whole?
- What can I do as a leader for you?

- Is this something you would be committed to long-term, or are you just looking to be part of something for a short time, then move on to something else?

2. Review: After you learn the answers do not throw this information out. Go back and review these questions and answers periodically after you get to know each potential member. Identify whether or not the person is in alignment with your mission and whether they are a true asset to the leadership of your organization or not.

Keep in mind, though, that frequently people provide the answers they believe we want to hear and as we get to know them we learn their true personalities and motives. This can help you develop their skills and motivate them over time.

3. Select the members that fit: As you begin the selection process, remember that you cannot please all the people all the time. Nor should you try to. Your goal is to choose a group of leaders who closely reflect and represent your vision and who are dedicated to helping that vision come to light.

Take a look at the answers one more time as described in the review step and narrow the choices down until you get down to the

6 or 8 people required to fill your council positions.

Once you have made your final selections, call each new council member directly, notify them of their appointment, and welcome them to leadership.

The first time I did this, I was pleasantly surprised at how each of my leadership council members graciously received this information and how excited they were to serve with me.

Identifying Your Leadership Council Member's Skills and Attributes

"We know from our experience that it is easier to develop trust in another person or in a group if we believe that we can disagree, and we will not be abandoned or hurt for our differences. It is difficult to trust those who deny us the right to be ourselves." **- Susan Wheelan**

Something that was—and still is—important to me is knowing my team members' strengths and weaknesses as well as their characteristics, behaviors, beliefs, and attitudes. The better you know these things about a person the better you can inspire him or her and the more you can rely on them to act and perform as needed.

Getting to know people and their personal history can tell you why they are like they are. When you understand people the barriers come down and developing trust and building a team is easier. When your leadership council trusts one another and you, they will be more open with their beliefs and ideas without the fear of ridicule. When our true selves are exposed many actions of pretension and posturing are no longer needed.

People who better understand one another with good perceptions of each other are less likely to judge each other and more likely to give the benefit of doubt to one another.

Team building requires members to work beyond their comfort zone. Often members will need to look past their established social filters to get to know teammates. Working with one another can help break down barriers as people learn about each other. However each individual must be open to this. A closed or negative member can bring down the house and must change or be removed.

To Be or Not to Be... On a Team

"Talent wins games, but teamwork and intelligence wins championships." **-Michael Jordan**

No matter how great the individual council members might be, the TEAM must be great. The best "dream teams" have crumbled because the members did not work together.

Teams can fail because of a lack of leadership, lack of defined tasks and roles, personality conflicts, an unclear vision, poor communication, incompatibility, no accountability in place, and more.

For me, the one qualifying factor that cannot be overlooked is that council members must want to be on the council. Skills alone will not make great leadership. The dynamics of the relationships are also vital to success. Council members that want to help others and see them succeed as well as work for the success of the team are most desirable.

- While conduct should be professional, when a team structure is too formal this can restrict the spirit of your team. Our team structure is very relaxed; however, it is clear that relaxation does not denote non-productivity.

- Council members should show a genuine interest to work on each other's challenges and issues. Amazingly, my council members have become "brothers and sisters." We spend the time to speak to one another outside of business and have a real desire to be of service to each other, in all areas of our lives.

- Council members should be willing to be accountable for mistakes. I can certainly say that I have been blessed to attract a group of people who do not lead with their ego. If a mistake is made, it is almost immediately revealed by the respective council member, which allows us as a council to recover or make changes quickly as to not experience fallout.

The 'Teamitude'

From the very beginning you need to form the attitude you want for your team. This starts with you. See, I had to BE the leader I wanted to also attract and work with. Therefore, I had to display the attitude that I wanted reflected in my team as well as in the individual attitudes I wanted team members to have.

All of your policies and procedures, principles, vision or mission statements, website content, communications, and speaking opportunities must come from and relay the attitude you want for your team. Attitude trickles down.

Something that remains a constant within my organization is that we take the time to publicly congratulate individual council members for jobs well done. We post it on Facebook or mention it on a live call or in an email. However, do not allow any member to take more credit than due. No matter how talented a member might be, remind your council that teamwork is the most important.

Defining Conflict

"The better able team members are to engage, speak, listen, hear, interpret, and respond constructively, the more likely their teams are to leverage conflict rather than be leveled by it." **- Runde and Flanagan**

Healthy debating is a valuable exploratory process. Debating initiates ideas and helps develop them. Teams need a healthy atmosphere to debate while supporting the fact that debating is not about fighting. While challenging and defending beliefs and positions is part of debating, discussions should not include personal attacks; everyone is on the same team.

Like a family, my team's leadership council has its disagreements too. And you know what, we get through them. As the leader, I make it a point to listen carefully to all sides then look for the commonality in each position so as to offer — and hopefully administer — a healthy consensus.

Honestly, sometimes it works and sometimes it doesn't...well, not always right away.

There are times when our council may be in disagreement. After taking a bit of time where I may speak with each member personally if needed, we are able to overcome the challenge.

When all else fails, I encourage them to remember the

mission and proceed from that space.

That usually does the trick.

Nonetheless, debating is beneficial when conducted as an exploratory fact-finding mission. Each side presents its case and the group votes. You then want to encourage all council members to embrace the outcome. You can have each member express his/her ideas for implementing the decision and reaching goals. This requires the losing side to take the opposite stance and get on board with the decision. You want no hard feelings when the members exit the discussion.

Creating an environment that enables authentic and healthy conflict will require work. Establishing a team charter agreement about how to deal with conflict can help.

Involve council members in creating the ground rules for behavior and expectations for debating. Remind everyone of the charter before debates.

When Someone Hits Below the Belt

If you are developing a winning leadership council, then members will be passionate. During the heat of debate, people often step on other's feelings unintentionally or with a direct personal attack.

Because you are cultivating a healthy environment and atmosphere of trust you will need to encourage team members to get past such incidents. The meeting should not be adjourned until any and all hurt feelings have been addressed. Your members need to apologize, forgive, and move on.

Debates should be reserved for issues that require the consideration of your entire leadership council. Your leadership council members might need to be encouraged to practice trust and mutual respect and how to know when other members are uncomfortable or angry regarding ideas. Debates should refrain from members ganging up on anyone or ignoring any dissenters. You want to encourage opposing views, not quash them. There should be no penalties or ridicule for disagreement.

Embrace Accountability

"Each day you are leading by example. Whether you realize it or not or whether it's positive or negative, you are influencing those around you." — **Rob Liano**

Most of us want for others to see ourselves in the best light possible. From childhood we cast blame on others as armor against appearing less than great. As adults, shifting the blame to others or events can erode our credibility with the people around us.

Setting an example of accountability and expecting the same from others will strengthen your team. When people are accountable they are empowered over situations rather than feeling or appearing as a victim.

I'll share more on this concept later and how it can be achieved not just through your leadership council, but throughout your entire organization as well.

Team Commitment

"Individual commitment to a group effort - that is what makes a team work, a company work, a society work, a civilization work." **- Vince Lombardi**

The level of success your leadership council achieves will be directly related to each member's level of commitment. While council members must be committed to the vision, goals, and core values of your team, they will frequently disagree with general consensus decisions. Commitment can be measured by their willingness to stick with a team decision despite their personal opinion or disagreement.

Your leadership council members should be able to make team projects and challenges their own and commit to them. This type of commitment is developed over time in a core foundation based on trust and encouragement and by involving all leadership council team members in the decision making process from the beginning and at all times. This will give members a stake in the team building and make commitment more likely.

We personally achieve this through use of our Team Leadership Council Facebook group.

In between council meetings (which I will discuss in just a

moment), ideas are sure to pop up. When that happens, we have created an environment where members feel safe to post their ideas on the group wall.

What this does is allow us to participate in each other's ongoing visions, which helps to solidify an even greater commitment to the team and its development.

If someone is offering ideas and proposed enhancements, many times that is a clear indication that you are working with someone who cares and plans on being around for awhile.

Set standards for your council and push them to achieve goals. Make your goals achievable. Communicate with your leadership council members often. Keep them in the loop or apprised of your activities and events.

You want to be a leader and meeting facilitator, not a micromanager. Ask for opinions, suggestions, and ideas. Keep your leadership council engaged. Allow your team to develop naturally and remind them of your purpose. You are there to assist them, and they are there to assist one another and other members not on the leadership council. Help your leadership council members become leaders by letting them lead.

Meetings

Set bi-monthly teleconferencing meetings for your leadership council like I have. Plan these ahead to increase the likelihood that everyone can attend. Keep the meetings to the point and on schedule. Give your team something valuable at each meeting so they will not want to miss out.

Have each council member report on their area and relevant events or activities. Set time limits for each person and adhere to the schedule. When subjects come up for debate or vote, allow each person to provide input. When a decision is made by the team, swiftly implement the action.

Developing a High-Performance Council

Advancing your LC's performance requires developing team attributes. Your leadership council should trust and have confidence in one another. Each member should have a clear understanding of the team's purpose and mission and incorporate this into their daily activities with enthusiasm. Provide your leadership council with team goals and work one on one to develop individual goals.

Request your LC team members write down their goals and

document the actions they take to support and reach these goals.

Team members should understand their roles and take responsibility for reaching goals. Members should welcome differing views and perspectives.

Define Roles Clearly

Every team member's role must be clear, and members must know the roles of other team members as well. Assign roles with contemplation for each individual's abilities, skills, level of knowledge and expertise, yet make roles transferrable if the situation arises where this is needed.

Allow the team to make recommendations for defining and assigning roles. This will empower the team and give them a greater stake in the outcome and also make the team aware of specific talents of other team members.

6. Step Three:

Developing Your Core Identity

"Effective leadership is putting first things first.
Effective management is discipline, carrying it out." - **Stephen Covey**

Right out of the gate, I knew I wanted a certain feeling and vibe amongst my team and amongst the leaders. I knew that this type of identity had to be created, and it was up to me to craft it out.

I decided early on to tap into who I really was.

By nature, I am not a micro-manager. Neither was my mom. In fact, when she said to do something, she didn't go checking up behind me every step of the way. Instead, she simply checked that it was done after a specified period of time that she indicated and if it was done, awesome. If it wasn't, well there was trouble ahead.

Anyway, I wanted to be able to inspire people to take action as opposed to dictating that they do. I also wanted a self-serving team, an independent team, and one that knew they could count on me for direction but not for every little problem or challenge they faced on our journey together.

Therefore, I opted to be the leader I always wanted while using my management ability where required.

Here are some principles I have internalized and applied to help build an identity within my team that cultivates leaders, encourages growth, and breeds loyalty.

Leadership versus Management

"Management is doing things right; leadership is doing the right things." **- Peter F. Drucker**

Managing a business requires management skills. Leading a team or organization will necessitate leadership skills. There is a difference.

Management is about planning and getting things done. A manager delegates or assigns tasks and ensures business operations are maintained. While management is essential, management depends on great leadership.

Leadership is outside of the strategic elements of business and tasks. Leadership is about influence, motivation, guidance, innovation, and people. A leader can also manage but must be able to step out of the management role to encourage action that achieves projects in line with the vision for the team and business. Leadership concerns the abilities and character of the leader. A leader must motivate and inspire people to accomplishments.

There are many great managers who can manage business, analyze operations, create strategies and visions, and coordinate finances. These people are much needed. Yet many do not influence anyone. They are not developed leaders. Developing leadership skills involves a commitment of time and energy. Leadership is often difficult to quantify while management results are easy to quantify. Leadership is an attitude and measure of influence.

A manager delegates tasks that must be accomplished by other people. A leader has or creates a vision, and must realize that vision working *through* other people by influencing and inspiring them.

Servant Leadership

"The servant-leader is servant first. It begins with the natural feeling that one wants to serve. The conscious choice brings one to aspire to lead. The best test ... is this: Do those served grow as persons? Do they, while being served, become healthier, wiser, freer, more autonomous, more likely themselves to become servants?" - Robert K. Greenleaf

Leaders that are strictly dictatorial bosses are becoming the dinosaurs of today's leadership model. Leaders that work to empower team members to become leaders, practice integrity, and involve team members in the decision making process are proving far more effective.

Robert K. Greenleaf is the innovator of the servant leadership model. He explains that the basis of servant leadership is about a leader who serves the team and people he or she leads. The team members are not seen as instruments to achieve a purpose but as the purpose.

The servant leader works to meet the needs of the team members and encourages them to reach their full potential. This type of leader works to serve the team before leading, without being dominating and utilizing power or force. Instead, this leader influences others to inspiration. While servant leadership is about serving the team, this leader does not take orders from them.

The Ten Attributes of the Servant Leader

"The key to successful leadership is influence, not authority." - **Kenneth Blanchard**

In *The Servant Leader Within,* Larry C. Spears, CEO of the Robert K. Greenleaf Center for Servant-Leadership, describes the ten attributes or skills the servant leader:

1. **A Servant Leader is a Good Listener.** Be completely committed to listening to your leadership council (LC) so that you understand them as a group as well as individuals. Only by listening to your LC team members can you understand and meet their needs.

2. **Servant Leaders are Empathetic.** Empathy does not equate to feeling sorry for someone, as many people believe. Empathy is about understanding others so that you can believe in them and see their true intentions even when they are not meeting your expectations. You can then point out and help them correct behaviors without talking down to or simply rejecting them.

3. **A Servant Leader is a Healer.** Working to understand and forgive others is a powerful tool for transformation.

4. **Servant Leaders are Aware.** Being aware of others and their needs will help the servant leader better serve and lead. The servant leader also works to develop a keen self-awareness.

5. **The Servant Leader is Persuasive.** Influence and inspiration are the tools of persuasion for the servant leader.

6. **Servant Leaders can conceptualize.** You need to see past the daily tasks and events of business and life to focus on the big picture. While short-term goals require attention, maintain a conceptual view of your vision and mission.

7. **Servant Leaders have Great Foresight.** By being aware, conceptualizing, being a good listener, and empathetic, you can develop your ability to predict the likely outcome of situations.

8. **The Servant Leader is a Steward.** Servant leaders are stewards for the greater good of the team, individuals, and society.

9. **Servant Leaders are Devoted to the Growth of their People.** A servant leader nurtures the personal, professional, and spiritual growth of the team and members.

10. **The Servant Leader Works to Build Community.** The servant leadership builds a sense of community for the team.

Wants versus Needs

Ask any parent and they will tell you there is a great difference between "wants" and "needs." Children often want things that are not the best for them or even healthy. While distinguishing the difference between wants and needs for children is commonly obvious, making this same distinction for your team and individuals is not always easy.

There is a major difference between the definitions:

want v.

1. To have a strong desire for; to have an inclination to

2. To wish or demand the presence of

need n.

1. A legitimate physical or psychological requirement for the health and welfare of human beings

You will never be able to fulfill all the "wants" of others. Plus, giving people everything they want is not great leadership or even advisable. You must decide what is best for everyone. The servant leader must often sacrifice his or her wants — or the wants of others — to meet the needs of the team.

Leadership Styles

There are a number of leadership styles, as well as leadership skills. Anything less than leading by example will erode your team. Hypocrisy is not a leadership style.

Demonstrate to your team that you are willing to take risks with them, to allow them the freedom to choose and make mistakes.

No matter how great your leadership skills you will eventually fail without this one attribute: integrity.

Leadership is about the person, not personality. Leadership skills and styles can be developed. There have been great leaders with different personalities and styles. Think about the differences between:

- Presidents Reagan and Kennedy
- Martin Luther King and Malcolm X
- Mother Teresa and the Dalai Lama
- Generals Eisenhower and Patton

All of these leaders were celebrated for their abilities to lead, yet each had outstandingly different leadership "styles." These leaders had incredible abilities to persuade and inspire followers to realize epic accomplishments.

Practice Great Leadership

"Leadership is the art of getting someone else to do something you want done because he wants to do it." **- Dwight D. Eisenhower**

Lead from the front with servant leadership and listen to the needs of your team. When you commit to meeting a need do what you say. Show others how you produce results by example.

Generate results and be the example for your organization. Produce more than the requirement and exceed expectations. This will inspire others to do the same. Stay in growth mode and be aware of yourself and your actions. Remain humble and give credit to your team for accomplishments. Practice servant leadership and teach your team to fish rather than fishing for them.

Be open to ideas from others and welcome their feedback. By respecting their opinions and expertise you will inspire respect. Be careful not to be a know it all. Rather than cutting people off when you might think that what they are saying is incorrect, allow them to keep talking and listen. You will learn much more than if you silence them. You can always educate people later.

Edify those who contribute to team growth and delegate implementation to the person who had the idea.

When an individual does not support the team vision, your job is to inspire and motivate them to embrace the vision. If they have an idea that is not aligned with the team vision, you will need to make an executive decision. When executive decisions need to be made, you must become comfortable when saying 'no' is required.

Openly display how much you sincerely care about others, your team, and your vision. Be generous about giving awards and recognition for accomplishments. Thank your team members often and publicly whenever possible. Bring them on stage and acknowledge their accomplishments. These actions cost you nothing yet can be valuable investments in your team.

For those deserving, go over and beyond. Treat your team like a loving family; Keep private matters private and do not betray the confidentiality.

Always encourage your team to keep going and never quit. Help your team by teaching them how to help themselves. Do not hand-hold and provide the answer to every request. Remember the differences between wants and needs. Push your team to problem shoot for themselves and they will learn how to solve problems.

Success is an individual choice and you are not responsible for the success or failure of others. While your leadership can support and empower them, the ultimate failure or success of others is in their hands.

Have positive expectations of your group and always lead with a belief in the best of intentions from them. Provide the platform to share expertise with others.

Empower your team. Identify those getting results and allow them to lead webinars and/or trainings to teach what is working for them. Let people be free to produce within the scope of the team vision. Build leaders and they will be loyal.

Foster a true networking environment and encourage support and gathering of local members to build.

Encourage local members to utilize available resources to grow and support presentations not controlled by you. This creates a bond inside the overall team and lowers attrition while promoting teamwork and initiative. This will inspire other leaders to lead in their respective locales and builds hubs inside of geographic areas which set the stage for areas of team presence and domination.

7. Step Four:
Marking the Territory

"A brand that captures your mind gains behavior. A brand that captures your heart gains commitment." - **Scott Talgo**

Choose a Team Name

Everybody wants to identify with something and be a part of something, especially in the world of network marketing. Therefore, I knew that in order to build something greater than myself, we needed a team name. I wanted the name to be reflective of our core identity, and one that was timeless rather than trendy.

I chose to stay away from personal name branding, because I didn't feel in my heart that "Team Tracey" or "The Tracey Walker Team" would be strong enough for others to want to market, attach themselves to long-term, promote or publicly claim membership of. Not because that name wasn't good enough, but because I expected leaders to develop and emerge. In keeping with that, I knew that other leaders within the team would eventually stray away from "the core" team and create one branded to themselves. Although that sounds good, it dilutes the power of what the team could be if we were all ranting and raving about ONE name and ONE brand.

I was careful to consider the ages, creeds, colors, and religions of my members. Once we had a few name choices, I brought them to the LC and we voted and agreed on our name, The Dream Team!

[1]Choosing a team name is an important step in the team building process. Not only should you pick a name that reflects your brand identity, but you also need to ensure it can be embraced by the ever-growing team for the long term. You should also give a thought to whether it's web-ready. Is the domain name available?

Here are some tips to help you pick, register, and protect your team name.

Factors to Consider When Naming Your Team or Business

Many businesses start out as freelancers, solo operations, or partnerships. In these cases, it's easy to fall back on your own name as your business name. Stay away from using your personal name for your team name.

Think about how your name will look in print and on the web. What connotations does it evoke? Is your name too corporate or not corporate enough? Does it reflect your philosophy and culture? Does it appeal to your market?

---

[1] http://www.sba.gov/content/how-name-business

Is your name unique? Pick a name that hasn't been claimed by others, online or offline. A quick web search and domain name search (more on this below) will alert you to any existing use.

Check for Trademarks

Trademark infringement can carry a high cost for your business. Before you pick a name, use the U.S. Patent and Trademark Office's trademark search tool to see if a similar name, or variations of it, is trademarked.

Pick a Name that is Web-Ready

In order to claim a website address or URL, your team name needs to be unique and available. To find out if your business name has been claimed online, do a simple web search to see if anyone is already using that name. I use GoDaddy.com to run url availability searches all the time. You can also do this using the WHOIS database of domain names. If it is available, be sure to claim it right away.

Claim Your Social Media Identity

It's a good idea to claim your social media name early in the naming process, even if you are not sure which sites you intend to use. A name for at least your team Facebook group should be set up.

Design a Team Logo

Select the colors for your logo and delegate the design to a graphics person on your leadership council if you have one. If you have a concept idea, share it with your LC. You can also outsource for design submissions and choose the one that best fits your purpose. Have your leadership council vote on their favorite one. You can also make revisions until you have your logo right.

Consistent Branding

Create items and apparel with your logo on it that your team can wear or use and make it available for purchase on your Ning site.

Coordinate attire for wearing to company events or team masterminds to be unified. Encourage team pride and as the leader, be a proud wearer of your logo and apparel first. This shows people you believe in what you are doing and alerts outsiders to the fact that your team is a real organization to be taken seriously.

Always reference your team name and logo in your marketing. Leverage the exclusivity of your team as a recruiting point. Share photos and videos from events displaying your team wear. Post testimonials referencing members of the team. This makes members feel they are a part of something special and provides the concept of strength and support in numbers.

8. Step Five: Devising the Basic Plan of Action

"Setting a goal is not the main thing. It is deciding how you will go about achieving it and staying with that plan." - **Tom Landry**

The Fast-Start Guide

New reps need a place to start. Drawing upon my previous experience with the "Lone-star" reps, I really wanted new members to have a road map, a fast start guide if you will.

So, the LC met and we decided that a fast start guide was in order. I sat down and thought about the processes in our particular business and environment. I asked myself questions like: "What is the very first thing a new member would need to do to get started?" "What terms or jargon do we use that may need to be defined for someone who is completely new to the industry?" "What basic setup is required before any marketing should take place?" And so on.

From that foundation, I created a10-step, fast start training guide that lists our most important initial activities. And as each new member joins our team, they are expected to complete those 10 steps accordingly. Not only does this build confidence in the new rep as they complete each step, but it boasts duplication.

In doing this for your team, remember that your foundation of integrity, empowerment, and dissemination of knowledge is essential. Therefore, your team will also need simple to follow instructions to get started. Break each activity down to the finest point then prioritize the list of activities. Next, test your list for accuracy. Enlist your leadership council to test the list and ask for feedback. When you are confident in your list, post your steps on your Ning site under a tab labeled "Start Here."

Identify IPAs (Income Producing Activities) and produce training videos. Teach them the most important income producing activities and maybe some of the intricacies of the free marketing and paid marketing strategies available.

When creating your training videos, keep them basic. You cannot train everything. Do not even try to, regardless of how compelled you feel to do so. Always point people back to these trainings for reference when questions arise as opposed to you answering them specifically.

When you create an environment of duplication and consistency where everyone is doing the same thing, you are in turn developing "a system." And once they know how this system works, and it's proven to be effective, it can become the heartbeat of the team. Nonetheless, allow room for others on the team to enhance these trainings and expound upon them as you grow.

Goals

Develop and share the blueprint to reaching goals. Identify the core commitments needed to reach goals. Break down actions and tasks needed by setting daily goals. Share the actual formula that produces the results you speak of and solidify the process by producing results from the formula yourself and sharing them. Reiterate how easy the blueprint is and be clear about the results expected.

In our business, the founders crafted out the 8-core commitments for all company members to practice daily, a huge plus. In this industry, you don't find founders doing that very often. They also set the productions goal, which is to sign up two new customers/affiliates daily. In fact, after the first 60-90 days of the company being in existence, data was pulled and compared to identify the similarities amongst those who had produced and earned the most over that period of time.

Those specifics were analyzed and became the formula we all used to duplicate those results. I, in turn, took that formula, wrote it out so that a baby could understand it, and made it available on our team site for all to be aware of.

Now, whenever someone asks what they must do specifically to get a particular outcome, anyone on our team can simply point them to that formula for them to review, follow and amend to achieve the specific result they desire.

Goals should be clear, concise, and measurable. You want to be able to see your progress and keep your activities on schedule to meet your goals. On our team, we have what we call a DMO, Daily Method of Operation. It varies from person to person of course, yet encouraging the team to literally write out and plan what they will do each day is what makes it measurable.

Be sure to write goals down and post the list where you will see it every day. There is a psychological association that happens when we write — and are reminded of — our goals daily. Recording your goals gives them more psychological weight.

Observe/Listen for Additional Needs

You should conduct brainstorming sessions with your leadership council to get recommendations and ideas for goals and ongoing training. Encourage participation from your developing leaders, too, and listen to every idea. Don't shoot anything down. Rejection can stop the flow of ideas. Remind your team to check their egos at the door.

When a new idea is accepted, implement enhancements quickly, and notify the team of and changes, revisions, or additions. Publicly edify the contributors.

This component has been key in development of the Dream Team. We always keep in mind that as the team grows, other needs may arise and enhancements may be required. As the leader of the team, I never claim to know everything or have all the answers. I must remain open to others' ideas and suggestions. Likewise, the culture has been created where others love to share what they are experiencing and expressing what they believe may be needed additionally. Change is inevitable and must be embraced. We encourage ideas to be brought forth from the team as a whole as well, not just the leadership council, and they know that if what they propose is value added and can sustain itself over time, it has a great chance of being adopted. This helps the team to grow together and not so much apart.

Create Supplemental Trainings

You cannot teach new members everything in a fast start training guide. So, identify which additional trainings are necessary for production and delegate these trainings to your team utilizing their expertise.

The Dream Team has a gold-mine of talent, and many of our team members know things I have no idea about. Therefore, whenever we want to create new content or enhance what we have, we look to our team to seek out who has the expertise in that area and ask them for their input.

Once they contribute, we celebrate them across the entire team and NEVER take credit as a council for what a valued member has contributed.

Involving your team will help you build a well-rounded curriculum. This also creates a platform for these leaders to build their brands and will encourage loyalty from your council as well as throughout your entire organization.

Create a FAQ Section

In my opinion, too many reps spend too much time answering instructional questions from their newest associates. Not only does this drain of energy and diminish passion, it wastes time and reduces productivity. By identifying the questions you get asked most often and polling the team, you can develop a list of Frequently Asked Questions.

We did this almost from the very beginning of the formation of our team. Each time I was asked a question more than twice, I wrote it down with its corresponding answer and posted it to the FAQ section of our team site.

As new questions were revealed they were added to the list as well until we had almost every possible question answered.

Now let me disclose something here. I did not sit down ahead of time and try to come up with questions or create them out of thin air on my own. I simply allowed the questions to be asked first from the team and began to develop the list from there.

After you develop your list with answers, create a FAQs tab on your Ning site. Notify all members about this and when asked questions you can simply refer them there.

Develop explicit answers to explicit questions. Update and add to this list as needed.

Take Action

"A real decision is measured by the fact that you've taken a new action. If there's no action, you haven't truly decided." **- Tony Robbins**

And that's all that really needs to be said about that!

Develop Habits for Success

"Successful people are simply those with successful habits." **- Brian Tracy**

Habits can help us reach our goals sooner and with less effort. As excited as you might be about reaching your goals don't start out by trying to make big changes immediately. Habits are formed over weeks. A common belief is that habits take 21 days to form. Choose a habit such as starting your day with a certain task and practice this for 21 days.

Plan for Mentors and Role Models

The majority of successful people have had considerable help to get where they are. A mentor can provide you with invaluable information from experience, guidance, and help making decisions. There are varying forms of mentoring from in person meetings and phone calls to email communications.

God knows I have had my share of mentors, and I am so thankful to them and for them.

If it weren't for Daegan Smith, I would have never understood how to automate myself and my business using tools such as a blog, a lead capture page, or an autoresponder.

If it weren't for Sheri Sharman, I would never have believed a woman could earn 6-figures a month in this industry and remain kind and humble.

If it weren't for Mark Hoverson, I would not have began to learn the process of how to sell from the stage, or in a breakout room for maximum sales and results.

If it weren't for Cedrick Harris, I would've never learned the one phrase that helped me to start closing twice as many sales on the phone (during the time in my career when I actually called prospects).

If it weren't for Jeffrey Combs, I would not have realized that at that time in my life, I was self-sabotaging my success and was a co-dependent. Me being awakened to this allowed me to make changes in my life, my thought processes, and in my behaviors to where my income sky-rocketed. I stopped holding myself back.

There are many more I could name; however, I simply wanted to demonstrate for you that all leaders have mentors, for various reasons at various times, including me.

As you continue as the leader of your team and seek guidance from time to time, look for people who exemplify the ethics, attitudes, virtues, and successful habits you are trying to develop. Look for a person you respect. Find mentors who are in positions you want to be in, those that have "been there, done that."

Establish the reason you are seeking a mentor and what you expect a mentor to do for you. Define your leadership and communication style and describe what kind of mentor would work best for you. Seek a mentor who has practiced servant leadership. Choose a mentor that encourages and inspires you, not attempts to control or judge you.

Test the water. Before requesting a person to become your mentor, ask advice on a singular issue or topic, and be prepared to pay for their time and advice...whatever it is. Always remember that critical and life changing information is not free. The biggest problem I see is that in home-based business, people want advice from top earners and leaders for free, and almost seem to expect it. Whereas in comparison, that is usually never the case when you visit a doctor's office as an office visit fee is required. Be respectful and considerate and do not demand anything. Once your proposed mentor responds, evaluate how they delivered the advice and how you felt. Ask yourself if you were you inspired and did the advice help?

When you do enlist a mentor, express your gratitude and give them honest feedback about any action you did or did not take based on their advice. Look for ways you can pay back your mentor or return the favor.

Do not develop dependency on your mentors. They are temporary and should be encouraging you to be independent.

Plan for Self Development

Personal development is much more than working on your attitude. You must continuously educate yourself to increase your knowledge and improve your skills. Set aside time for self development and seek out courses and webinars to attend that support the skills and knowledge needed to reach your goals.

On our team we have what we call "the playbook." The playbook lists out and explains what should be done daily. However, there are two plays inside our playbook that relate to personal development: 1) to read for at least 1-hour DAILY and 2) to listen to a personal development audio for at least 15-minutes DAILY.

All members of the Dream Team are expected to work harder on themselves than they do in their businesses. It is our culture to do so and hold members accountable for such.

After all, nothing feels better than investing in yourself.

9. Step Six:

Supporting the Troops

Motivating Your Team

"Of course motivation is not permanent. But then, neither is bathing; but it is something you should do on a regular basis." - **Zig Ziglar**

Most anybody can be motivated for a few minutes. The trick is getting your team to stay motivated. The enthusiasm that was there at the beginning of joining the team can erode with time. People get distracted and tired. Poor leadership, arguments, disorganization, and other problems can cause passion to wane. Because of that you will need to know how to motivate your team when things seem hopeless and people are feeling down.

I remember a time when our company was just getting started and we faced merchant processing issues. In other words, we had no unified and sustainable way to receive payments from new customers/affiliates, nor could we pay the affiliates in the company for their production.

It was a time where morale was low and complaining was starting to spread like a virus.

I made up my mind right then and there that our founders were going to find a solution, no matter how long it took.

From that space, I set a new tone to the group and vocally expressed how we as a team would proceed.

- Complaining was not allowed
- The use of words like "overwhelmed" and "confused" were banned

- Focus was required

- Blogging daily, regardless of any of the corporate challenges, was to be done

- The daily motivational calls became more inspirational to help people commit and stay in the game

And this is to just name a few of the things we did to keep the team motivated when all hell seemed to be breaking loose.

Then once resolution was attained, we all looked back at how awesome it was to fight through during that time and to come out on the other side victorious.

So, learn all the ways that motivate people and learn what motivates each team member. Things like independence, responsibility, recognition, security, camaraderie, feeling important, having friends and more can motivate people. There are many methods and strategies to keep your team motivated.

Here's how I accomplish this.

Motivate Yourself First

"If you don't FEEL enthusiastic, ACT enthusiastic. Soon, you'll BE enthusiastic. Double your enthusiasm and you'll probably double your income." **- Frank Bettger**

Enthusiasm is contagious. When people see your passion, they want some too. Getting others excited is much easier when you are excited.

If you are not enthusiastic, start *acting* enthusiastic. A great story about enthusiasm can be found in a book written long ago by the author of the quote above, Frank Bettger, titled *How I Raised Myself from Failure to Success in Selling.* You will find plenty of other great stories from Mr. Bettger in the book as well.

"Mastering others is strength. Mastering yourself is true power."
- Lao Tzu

When you are passionate about your team's goals, the team members will see more value in the goals. Use stories and examples to motivate your team instead of worn clichés. Stories are much more exciting and people relate to them. I recommend using stories from your own life and personal experiences. Your journey has value…share it.

Celebrate Success

Celebrate all successes openly in the group. These successes can be income generated, mindset shifts, ability to generate leads, new enrollments, strategies that now make sense, and overcoming obstacles such as fear.

In our team Facebook group, we celebrate the smallest things to the biggest. When someone gets their first sign up, we shout about it. When someone gets their first commission, we scream about it. When someone has "a light-bulb moment," we virtually hug them. When someone finally begins to believe, we embrace them. And so on. You should be doing this too!

Edify Leaders and Producers

Recognition is a strong motivator and trumps monetary reward for some people. Even if they originally join for the money, they often stay for the feeling. Recognizing successes provides insight on others successes and gives a platform for leaders to share, teach, and develop. These successes prove duplication is taking place and spawns confidence in others that they can do it too.

Not only do we do this in the virtual world, we do it live and in person at company events as well.

Make Examples Out of Team Heroes

Rather than being on the lookout for mistakes, be on the watch for 'things done right.' Let people know they did a good job and *thank* them. Appreciation is a rare commodity in the world, yet costs you nothing.

Identify and praise the team "hero" who saved the day. Train your team members to watch for quality work and praise one another. When outsiders see a group of people operating like this they will be beating on the door to find out how to join.

Create Daily Motivational Calls

Daily motivational calls demonstrate your passion and give you the opportunity to inspire your team. They unify your team and help them focus on the team vision. They become in touch with you and vice versa. Be consistent with your calls and messages. You will become the glue that holds the team together during challenging times, and these calls can make all the difference.

Our Dream Team daily calls are held EVERY Monday through Friday at 12 p.m. noon EST. And we do not skip or postpone them, except for a major holiday.

In fact, I invite you to jump on and listen to one of our Dream Team calls to see for yourself! The dial-in number is (760) 569-6000, pin: 589046#.

I personally used to deliver the message on each call each day for awhile. Then we decided to share the love by instituting a call schedule where each member of our leadership council would host the call on a particular day. That gave us the opportunity to connect with more members. If I was the only one speaking, I would only connect with those who were like me. However, with a large team, there are members who will more than likely resonate with someone else and someone else's story.

motivated. The days of calling your sponsor for everything are gone. This does not mean you cannot have mentors and other support, only that the ultimate decisions are now yours.

Respect that support is still necessary as this is a people business. Create a Skype chat and/or a private Facebook group for your entire team to participate in. Be an active contributor in these forums. Provide the freedom for others to contribute. These actions will create a family and a real team environment.

Cross Train Your Team Members

When you are working with larger groups, the one thing you will want to be able to do is to enlighten others at the same time that you might be coaching someone else.

Our Facebook group really assists with this. For example, someone may post a question where team members have the freedom to post their personal opinions and responses to the question.

If I go into the post and realize that someone offered "not so good" advice, or gave the improper information, my ability to correct, right there on the post, notifies ALL responders at the same time of the correct answer or directive.

What happens now is that you have empowered at least that group of commenters to go forth and share the correct information with others as that particular issue may arise again.

The difference is that I no longer have to respond that way every time; there is an army that can respond at any given time on behalf of the group.

Develop the "Win-Win" Philosophy

When you begin thinking about how the people around you can win, you will win too. People who practice the "win-win" philosophy attract other win-win, optimistic people and greatly grow their circle of influence.

A win-win leader demonstrates concern for others and listens to their wants and needs. A win-win leader looks for solutions to problems that everyone involved benefits from. [2]Win-win isn't about being nice, nor is it a quick-fix technique. It is a character-based code for human interaction and collaboration.

Most of us learn to base our self-worth on comparisons and competition. We think about succeeding in terms of someone else failing—that is, if I win, you lose; or if you win, I lose. Life becomes a zero-sum game. There is only so much pie to go around, and if

---

[2] Covey, Stephen; The 7 Habits of Highly Effective People

you get a big piece, there is less for me; it's not fair, and I'm going to make sure you don't get anymore.

We all play the game, but how much fun is it really?

Win-win sees life as a cooperative arena, not a competitive one. Win-win is a frame of mind and heart that constantly seeks mutual benefit in all human interactions. Win-win means agreements or solutions are mutually beneficial and satisfying. We both get to eat the pie and it tastes pretty darn good!

I've come to realize that a leader or organization that approaches conflicts with a win-win attitude possesses three vital character traits:

- Integrity: sticking with your true feelings, values, and commitments
- Maturity: expressing your ideas and feelings with courage and consideration for the ideas and feelings of others
- Abundance Mentality: believing there is plenty for everyone

Many people think in terms of either/or: either you're nice or you're tough. Win-win requires that you be both. It is a balancing act between courage and consideration. To go for win-

win, you not only have to be empathic, but you also have to be confident. You not only have to be considerate and sensitive, you also have to be brave. To do that—to achieve that balance between courage and consideration—is the essence of real maturity and is fundamental to win-win.

Leadership

[3]Over the past several years, one of the most important contributions psychology has made to the field of business has been in determining the key traits of acknowledged leaders. Psychological tests have been used to determine what characteristics are most commonly noted among successful leaders. This list of characteristics can be used for developmental purposes to help team leaders gain insight and develop their leadership skills.

The increasing rate of change in the business environment is a major factor in this new emphasis on leadership; whereas in the past, managers (in the corporate world) were expected to maintain the status quo in order to move ahead, new forces in the marketplace have made it necessary to expand this narrow focus. The new leaders and entrepreneurs of tomorrow are visionary.

---

[3] http://www.sba.gov/

They are both learners and teachers. Not only do they foresee paradigm changes in society, but they also have a strong sense of ethics and work to build integrity in their organizations.

I have done my best to be this type of leader within my organization and will continue to strive towards improvement.

Raymond Cattell, a pioneer in the field of personality assessment, developed the Leadership Potential equation in 1954. This equation, which was based on a study of military leaders, is used today to determine the traits which characterize an effective leader. The traits of an effective leader include the following:

- **Emotional stability**: Good leaders must be able to tolerate frustration and stress. Overall, they must be well-adjusted and have the psychological maturity to deal with anything they are required to face.

- **Dominance**: Leaders are often competitive, decisive and usually enjoy overcoming obstacles. Overall, they are assertive in their thinking style as well as their attitude in dealing with others.

- **Enthusiasm**: Leaders are usually seen as active, expressive, and energetic. They are often very optimistic and open to change. Overall, they are generally quick and alert and tend to be uninhibited.

- **Conscientiousness**: Leaders are often dominated by a sense of duty and tend to be very exacting in character. They usually have a very high standard of excellence and an inward desire to do their best. They also have a need for order and tend to be very self-disciplined.

- **Social boldness**: Leaders tend to be spontaneous risk-takers. They are usually socially aggressive and generally thick-skinned. Overall, they are responsive to others and tend to be high in emotional stamina.

- **Self-assurance**: Self-confidence and resiliency are common traits among leaders. They tend to be free of guilt and have little or no need for approval. They are generally unaffected by prior mistakes or failures.

- **Compulsiveness**: Leaders are controlled and very precise in their social interactions. Overall, they are very protective of their integrity and reputation and consequently tend to be socially aware and careful, abundant in foresight, and very careful when making decisions or determining specific actions.

- **Intuitiveness**: Rapid changes in the world today, combined with information overload, result in an inability to know everything. In other words, reasoning and logic will not get you through all situations. In fact, more and more leaders are learning the value of using their intuition and trusting their gut when making decisions.

- **Empathy**: Being able to put yourself in the other person's shoes is a key trait of leaders today. Without empathy, you can't build trust; without trust, you will never be able to get the best effort from your team.

- **Charisma**: People usually perceive leaders as larger than life. Charisma plays a large part in this perception. Leaders who have charisma are able to arouse strong emotions in their team by defining a vision which unites and captivates them. Using this vision, leaders motivate members to reach toward a future goal by tying the goal to substantial personal rewards and values.

Leaders are rarely (if ever) born. Circumstances and persistence are major components in the developmental process of any leader, so if your goal is to become a leader, work on developing those areas of your personality that you feel are not up to par. For instance, if you have all of the basic traits but do not consider yourself very much of a people person, try taking classes or reading books on empathy. On the other end, if relating to others has always come naturally to you, but you have trouble making logical decisions, try learning about tough-mindedness and how to develop more psychological resistance. Just remember, anyone can do anything they set their mind to.

10. Step Seven:
Expanding Beyond Measure

"Don't lower your expectations to meet your performance. Raise your level of performance to meet your expectations. Expect the best of yourself, and then do what is necessary to make it a reality." **- Ralph Marston**

Now that you have Steps 1-6 underway, over time, new leaders and success stories should be rising from within your team.

Your eyes should be open as the leader, and you should purposefully be looking for those members who are progressing through not only the training, but who are producing quantifiable results.

In my organization, I look for the people who have earned at least 5-figures within their business.

The reason is because if I have a team member who has made at least $10,000, then it is apparent that they understand at least the basics of the business, have enrolled some new reps, and that those new reps have enrolled some new reps. At this point, there is a solid foundation of a team forming.

In an effort to keep the duplication funneling throughout the team, it is pertinent that this new leader utilizes the same process I have shared with you here.

Step 7 is all about growing the team by sharing steps 1-6 with your core leaders and producers to allow them to build teams of high-performance as well, thus expanding the success of the overall team beyond measure.

It is in this step that I mentor and coach these members, from a leadership perspective, on how to simultaneously build successful, thriving, and loyal teams, just as I have.

In fact, the more leaders we have on the team who are duplicating the Ultimate Team Building Formula, the more reach we can have, the greater leverage we attain, and the more success we can create from the members within our organization.

In addition to teaching Steps 1-6 to the superstars emerging, here are some other critical components you'll need to make this formula even more powerful.

Form A Leadership Mastermind

With this new wave of leadership forming in the team, it is important that you pull these leaders together to form a leadership mastermind.

The purpose of this mastermind would be the equivalent to that of an "upper management" group inside of a corporation. To align all the different departments and bring them together so that each representative of each area is aware of what is going on outside their direct scope to provide insight on what's working and what's not working for the company as a whole.

In this environment, your leadership council serves as the Board of Directors for your group. But as new leaders develop, they will have their own LCs, yet you will want to work with these leaders closely to move the "umbrella" team forward with their input. This gives you access to each team leader and their expertise. It also makes good for involving those committed leaders with an even greater cause...the whole team.

Help Your New Team Leaders Set Long and Short Term Goals

Expanding beyond measure begins with goals for your team leaders and their members. Work closely with your team leaders to develop goals. Let every leader know they are responsible for achieving the team's goals as well as their own. Teach your leaders to recognize that when each member is working toward the team's goals, everyone will share in the success.

Work one on one as a mentor with your leadership mastermind to help them set and reach personal short and long term goals. These goals can be numbers (financial), as well as material things, milestones of achievement and projects or tasks and firing their bosses.

Your leadership mastermind should have internalized your vision so much that their language, actions, words, and goals coincide. Their choices, daily tasks, and attitudes should reflect the vision and work toward the goals. They should be sleeping, breathing, and eating the mission!

Trust and Believe In Your Mastermind

"Show people you believe in them and expect great things. Don't go overboard – just give them your honest appraisal." **– Frank Bettger**

Your leadership mastermind should have a clear picture of your goals and a system in place for achieving them. As you get to know them and their needs show them you have confidence in their abilities. Be there for support, motivation, and leadership, but make sure they know you believe in them. Encourage this same confidence and trust between team members as well. Be completely transparent and let them know exactly how to walk in your footsteps.

Develop Accountability

Create an environment of accountability for the leadership mastermind by having them document their production. Ask them to identify areas needing improvement.

Start by assuming you are wrong about every situation. This allows you to open your mind and hear what people are saying. This forces you to listen, ask questions, consider new ideas, and challenge your previous assumptions.

When we assume we know what people are going to say, we might listen but we do not hear. Listen to every person and treat what they are saying as if the conversation and issue is new and you do not have the answer.

Promote and Campaign

Each member of the leadership mastermind should be committed to promoting and campaigning for massive attendance at all company events. Events build belief by showing the system is working for others and solidifies commitment. The enthusiasm, leadership, and social proof keeps members engaged, recharged, and in the game. Additionally, it helps to release fears. Work to double attendance at each subsequent event.

Encourage Risk-Taking and Creativity

Give your leadership mastermind assignments that challenge them individually and as a team. Encourage them to be innovative and refrain from ridiculing their ideas or mistakes. Most people are afraid to take risks. Teach them how to surmise different outcomes and assess risks. Remind them to support each other in taking risks. A strong support system can enable individuals to excel. An empowered team will become more effective at making decisions and producing results.

Make Loyalty and Enthusiasm Priorities

Many team leaders expect enthusiasm to be a by-product of the team. Just like fires, enthusiasm must be started. You can start enthusiasm by displaying enthusiasm, and as previously discussed, acting enthusiastic.

However, take this one more step and make enthusiasm a priority. Enthusiasm should be at the top of your 'to-do' list every day and still evident at the end of the day.

Loyalty is another often neglected yet critical team ingredient. Find ways to instill, reinforce, and display loyalty to the team and what it stands for in every communication and action throughout your day. Move your team members from a mere understanding of your team's mission to a pledge of loyalty that shows through in their communications and actions also.

Develop A Consensus on Strategies, Tactics, and Resources

A great leader will develop ways to plan, communicate, and strategize with the inclusion of all leadership mastermind members. Allow all members to give input, feedback, and their opinions.

Encourage differing views to learn about team members, gain ideas, and choose actions. Teach your leadership mastermind differing viewpoints to spawn broader thinking and better ideas and answers. Members who are not intimidated to share their ideas can become very valuable. Then bring the team to a consensus on the plan of action.

Encourage your mastermind to stand behind all final decisions. Promote the sharing of all resources among all team members.

Use Mistakes as Opportunities

Mistakes, errors, and what some people refer to as failures are all great learning opportunities. Rather than seek or place blame for mishaps look for causes and future prevention. Teach your leadership mastermind to see any individual error as a team responsibility. This will open the door (and minds) for education. Your leadership can make all the difference in how your mastermind sees errors. When blame is no longer part of the equation, people will take the leap to seeking knowledge instead.

Change Criticism to Helpful Feedback

Teach your leadership mastermind how to offer one another help without criticism. One way is to always avoid any personal connection to the feedback. Begin feedback with a positive statement or praise. Make this about you instead of them. Offer feedback framed within what you learned or how you improved. This type of correcting will create trust and confidence on your team instead of resentment.

The Cure Starts at the Top

Every team will have members that exhibit political behavior that can threaten your team's performance. Team politics start at the top of the organization. Even minor arguments among those at the top will appear to be major wars to followers. When leaders display behavior such as back stabbing, one-up-man-ship, avoidance of conflict, gossiping, dishonesty, disloyalty, dislike, and selfishness then team members will do exactly what you want them to do... *mimic and follow!*

Allowing these behaviors to be displayed by those who need to be setting an example will result in decreased efficiency, high member turnover, and increased atrophy.

Building a team with a healthy and productive environment begins at the top with you and your leadership mastermind. Begin by setting an example for your leaders to follow. Practice strong self-discipline to be a successful role model. Make it clear to your leaders that detrimental behavior is not acceptable. The last thing you want is a team environment of dysfunction, disorganization, disillusionment, distrust, fatigue, and fracture.

When team members see the people at the top working together, overcoming differences, displaying example behavior, and working for the greater good of the team, they will be secure and more productive.

The Power of High Performance Teamwork

High performance teamwork is a sight to behold. Members are focused and working together for a greater purpose. They exhibit loyalty by supporting all group decisions and one another. They talk highly of their team, the members, and the leadership. They make decisions and adapt to changes quickly without losing focus.

When observed the high performance team seems almost telepathic. They see problems before they occur, generate solutions, and have an uncanny ability to read each other. They welcome each other's viewpoints and when they disagree, they refrain from personal attacks or passive aggressive behavior. They support the ultimate decision even when they were opposed.

While this might seem like a fantasy team, this is the team you are striving to create. While no team reaches perfection, the vision keeps us pushing in the right directions.

Duplicate

Show your leaders how to duplicate this exact system. Since this system works treat it as a franchise. Make sure your leadership council and leadership mastermind has this book and promotes duplication several levels down. This keeps teams within the team operating the same way and helps build familiarity and confidence because of the consistency of the message.

Then let them fly!

I personally feel as though we have created a "fantasy" team in the Dream Team utilizing the Ultimate Team Building Formula. It took me quite sometime to tweak and modify this formula so that it produced results.

Now that it is proven, I am excited to have had the opportunity to share this winning formula with you so that you too can create the team of your dreams.

If I was able to do it, so can you!

About the Author

Tracey Walker is an expert home-based business entrepreneur and internet marketer. In just a little over a year online, she became a leading force in the Network Marketing training industry and has achieved top producer/Top Female Income Producer status in both of the internet marketing programs she has chosen to be an affiliate of.

Prior to joining the home-based business arena, Tracey was a highly influential and successful real estate investor specializing in pre-foreclosures and negotiating short sales. It was the downturn in the market that was the catalyst in her being exposed to and participating in the network marketing industry.

During her first years in network marketing, Tracey was an offline presenter for her previous network marketing companies. In this role, she not only led her own organization, but also trained the core team in Chicago of over 2000 distributors. It was here where she honed in on coaching and training serious network marketers to be successful.